# CREEDENCE CLEARWATER REVIVAL
## FOR UKULELE

Cover photo © Pictorial Press / Cache Agency

ISBN 978-1-4950-0802-3

**HAL•LEONARD®**
CORPORATION

7777 W. BLUEMOUND RD. P.O. BOX 13819 MILWAUKEE, WI 53213

In Australia Contact:
**Hal Leonard Australia Pty. Ltd.**
4 Lentara Court
Cheltenham, Victoria, 3192 Australia
Email: ausadmin@halleonard.com.au

Visit Hal Leonard Online at
**www.halleonard.com**

# Bad Moon Rising

**Words and Music by John Fogerty**

*Additional Lyrics*

2. I hear hurricanes a-blowin'.
   I know the end is comin' soon.
   I fear rivers overflowin'.
   I hear the voice of rage and ruin.

3. Hope you got your things together.
   Hope you are quite prepared to die.
   Looks like we're in for nasty weather.
   One eye is taken for an eye.

# Commotion

**Words and Music by John Fogerty**

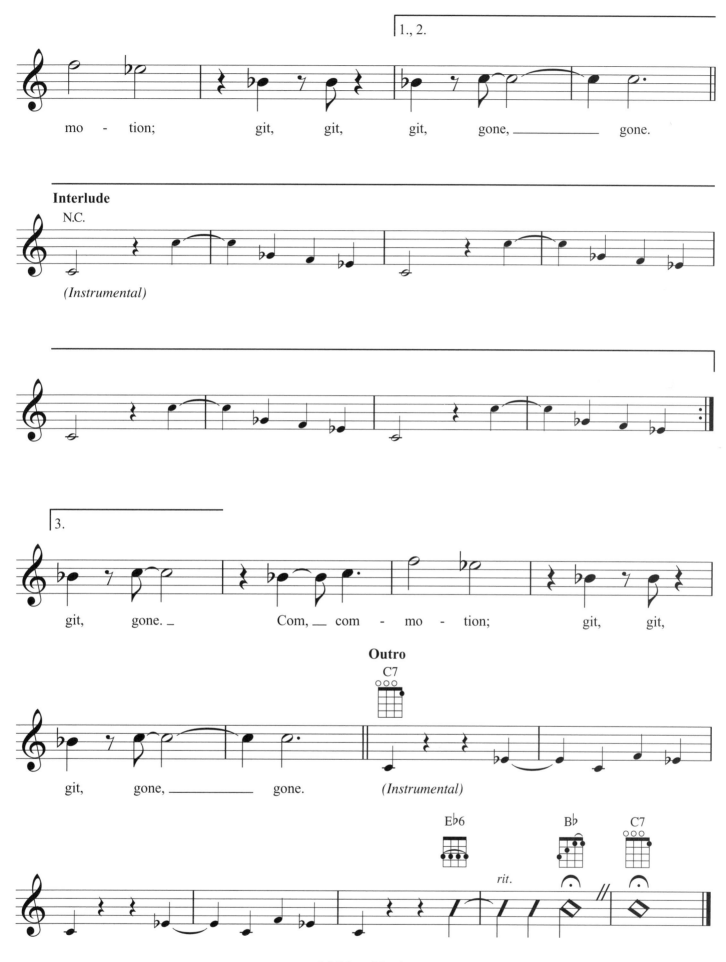

*Additional Lyrics*

2. People keep a-talkin'; they don't say a word.
   Jaw, jaw, jaw, jaw, jaw.
   Talk up in the White House, talk up to your door.
   So much going on, I just can't hear.

3. Hurrying to get there so you save some time.
   Run, run, run, run, run.
   Rushing to the treadmill, rushing to get home,
   Worry 'bout the time you save, save.

# Down on the Corner

**Words and Music by John Fogerty**

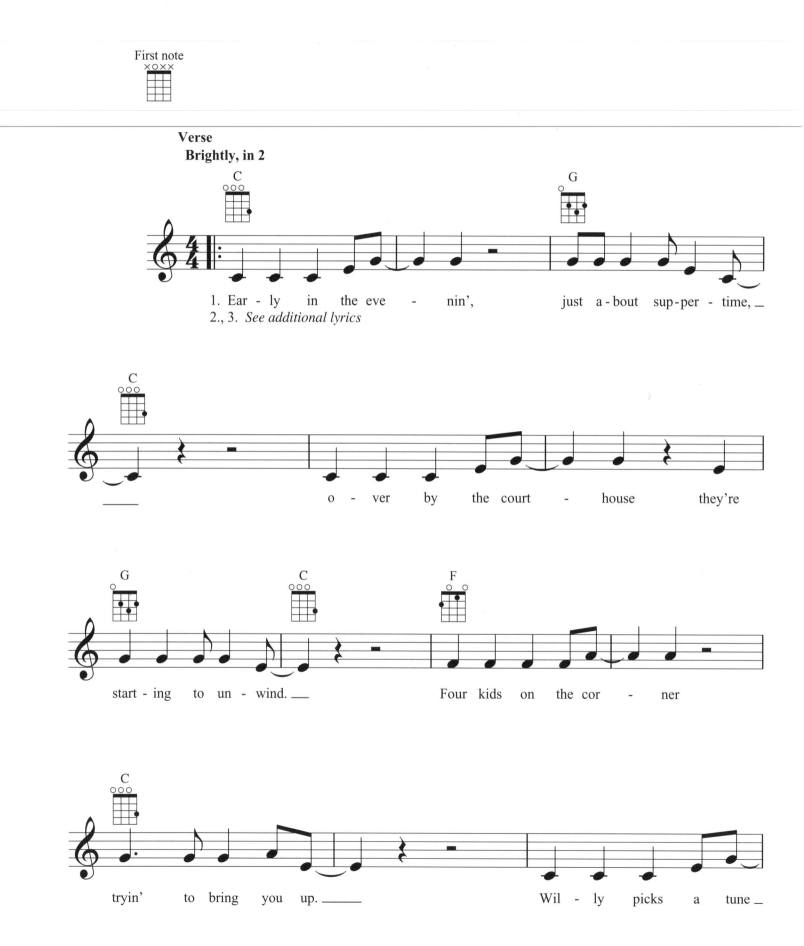

1. Ear - ly in the eve - nin', just a - bout sup-per - time, _
2., 3. *See additional lyrics*

_ o - ver by the court - house they're

start - ing to un - wind. _ Four kids on the cor - ner

tryin' to bring you up. _ Wil - ly picks a tune _

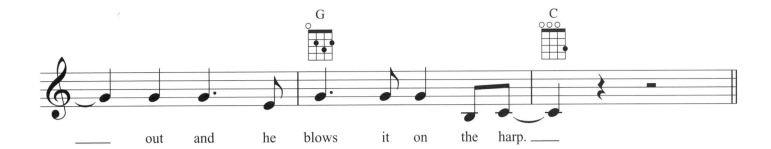

_____ out and he blows it on the harp. _____

**Chorus**

Down on the cor - ner, out in the street, _

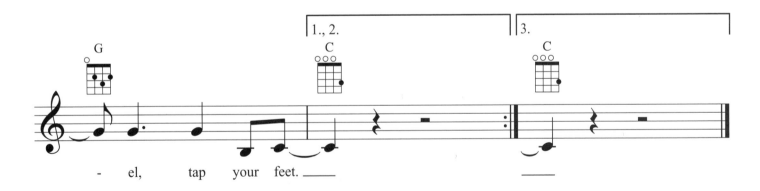

_____ Wil - ly and the Poor - boys are play - in'. Bring a nick-

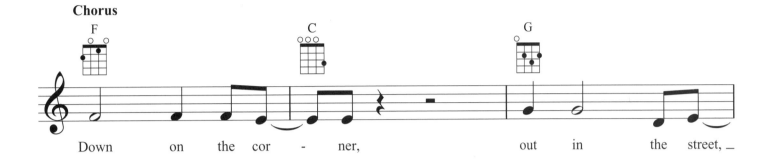

1., 2.

3.

- el, tap your feet. _____ _____

*Additional Lyrics*

2. Rooster hits the washboard and people just gotta smile.
   Blinky thumps the gut bass and solos for a while.
   Poorboy twangs the rhythm out on his kalamazoo.
   Willy goes into a dance and doubles on kazoo.

3. You don't need a penny just to hang around,
   But if you've got a nickel, won't you lay your money down?
   Over on the corner there's a happy noise.
   People come from all around to watch the magic boy.

# Fortunate Son

**Words and Music by John Fogerty**

**First note**

**Verse**
**Moderate Rock**

1. Some folks are born ___ made ___ to wave the flag.
2., 3. *See additional lyrics*

Ooh, they're red, white and blue. _____

And when ___ the band ___ plays "Hail _____ to the Chief,"

ooh, they point the can - non at you, Lord. ___

*Additional Lyrics*

2. Some folks are born silver spoon in hand.
   Lord, don't they help themselves!
   But when the tax man comes to the door,
   Lord, the house looks like a rummage sale.

*Chorus:*  It ain't me, it ain't me.
   I ain't no millionaire's son, no.
   It ain't me, it ain't me.
   I ain't no fortunate one, no.

3. Some folks inherit star-spangled eyes.
   Ooh, they'll send you down to war.
   And when you ask 'em, "How much should we give?"
   Ooh, they only answer, "More, more, more!"

*Chorus:*  It ain't me, it ain't me.
   I ain't no military son, son, no.
   It ain't me, it ain't me.
   I ain't no fortunate one, no.

# Born on the Bayou

**Words and Music by John Fogerty**

'cause he'll get you now, now."

**Verse**

G7

2. I can re - mem - ber the Fourth ___ of Ju - ly, ___
3. Wish I was back ___ on the bay - ou,

run - nin' through the back - wood bare. ___ And
roll - in' with some Ca - jun queen. ___

I can still hear ___ my old hound ___ dog bark - in', chas -
Wish - in' I were ___ a ___ fast ___ freight train, ___ just a -

*To Coda* ⊕

F C

- in' down a hoo - doo there, ___ chas -
choo - glin' on ___ down to New ___

G7

F C

- in' down a hoo - doo there. ___

**Chorus**

Born ___ on the bay - ou,

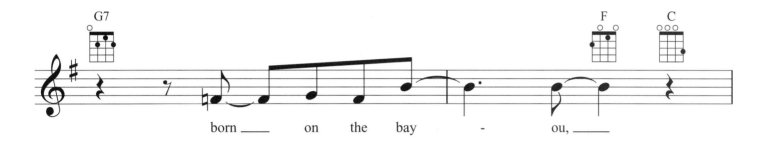

born ___ on the bay - ou, ___

born ___ on the bay - ou.

**D.S. al Coda**

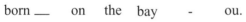

Coda

**Outro-Chorus**

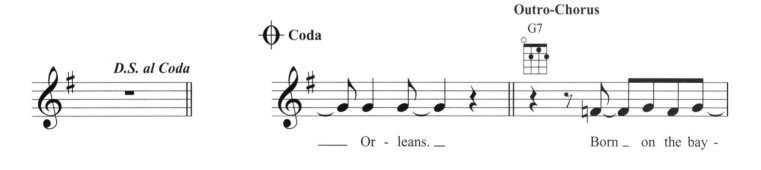

___ Or - leans. ___          Born _ on the bay -

- ou,          born ___ on the bay - ou, ___

born ___ on the bay - ou.

# Green River

**Words and Music by John Fogerty**

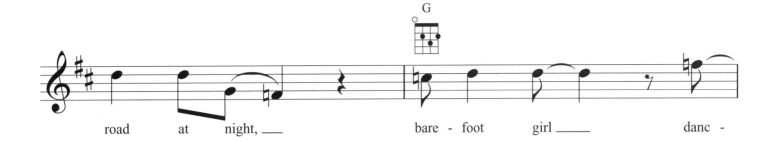

road      at      night, ___          bare - foot     girl ___       danc -

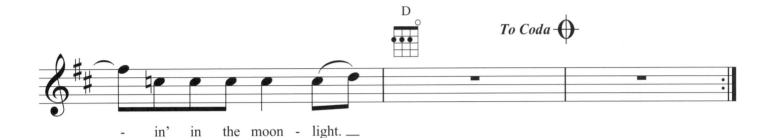

- in'    in    the    moon - light. ___

Well. _____       *(Instrumental)*

*(Instrumental)*

*Additional Lyrics*

2. I can hear the bullfrog calling me, oh.
     Wond'ring if my rope's still hangin' to the tree, oh.
     Love to kick my feet way down the shallow water.
     Shoo, fly, dragonfly, get back to your mother.
     Pick up a flat rock, skip it across Green River.

3. Up at Cody's camp, I spent my days, oh,
     With flatcar riders and crosstie walkers.
     Old Cody Junior took me over,
     Said, "You're gonna find the world is smould'ring,
     And if you get lost, come on home to Green River."

# Have You Ever Seen the Rain?

**Words and Music by John Fogerty**

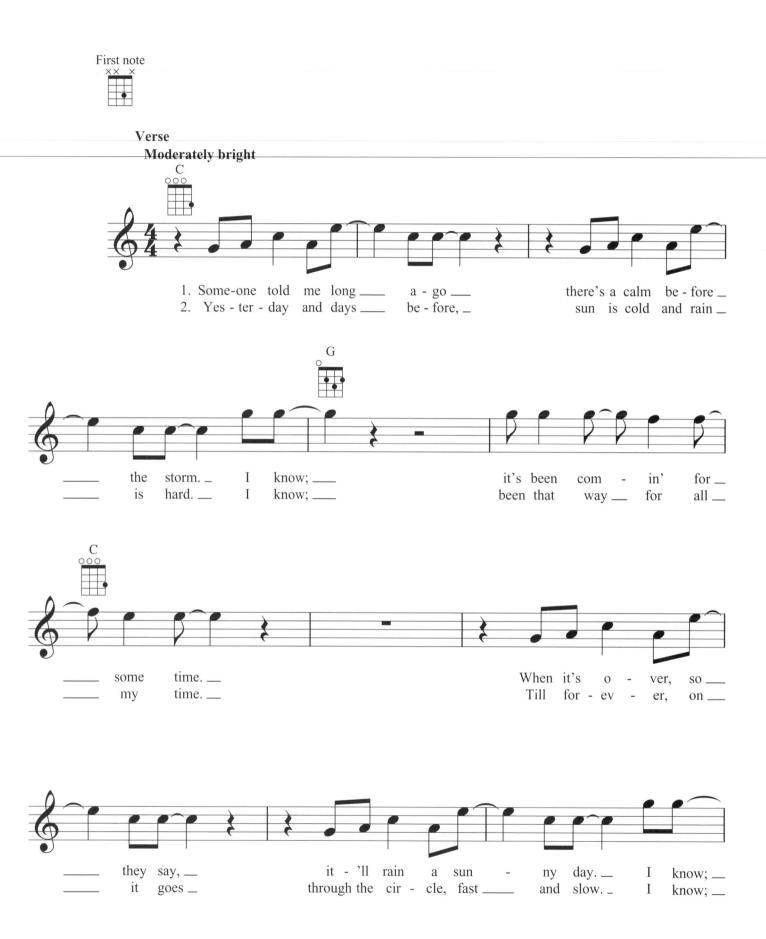

# Hey, Tonight

**Words and Music by John Fogerty**

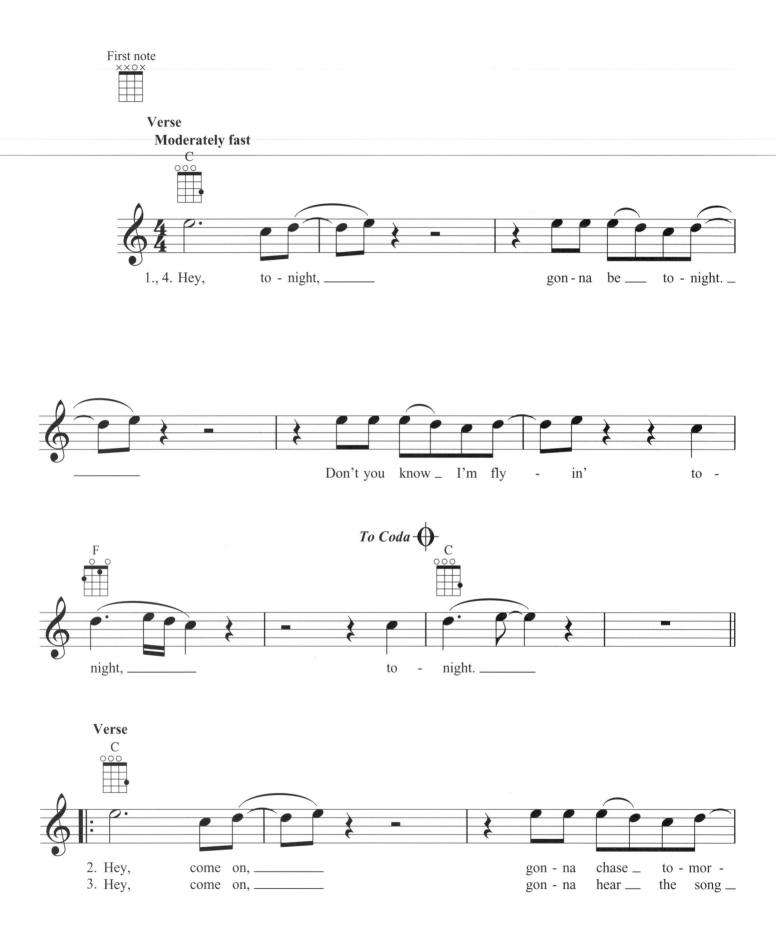

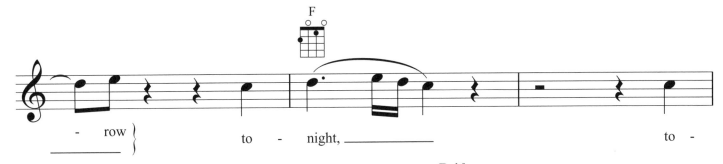

- row        to - night, _____        to -

**Bridge**

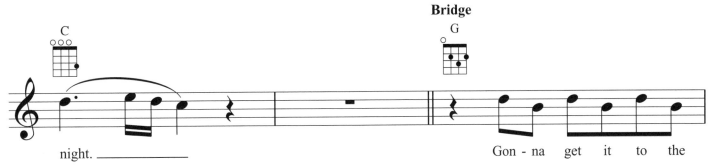

night. _____        Gon - na get it to the

raft - ers;        watch me now.        Jo - dy's gon - na get re -

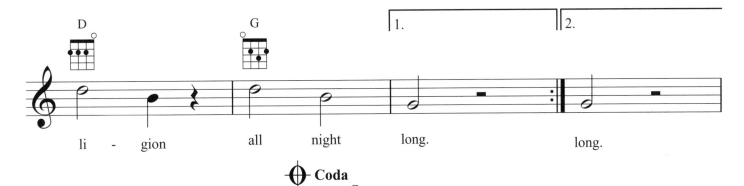

li - gion        all night long.        long.

*D.C. al Coda*

Oh!        night. _____        To -

**Outro**

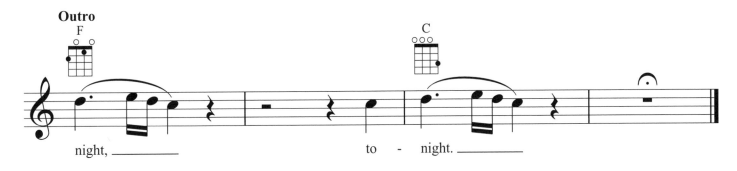

night, _____        to - night. _____

# I Put a Spell on You

**Words and Music by Jay Hawkins**

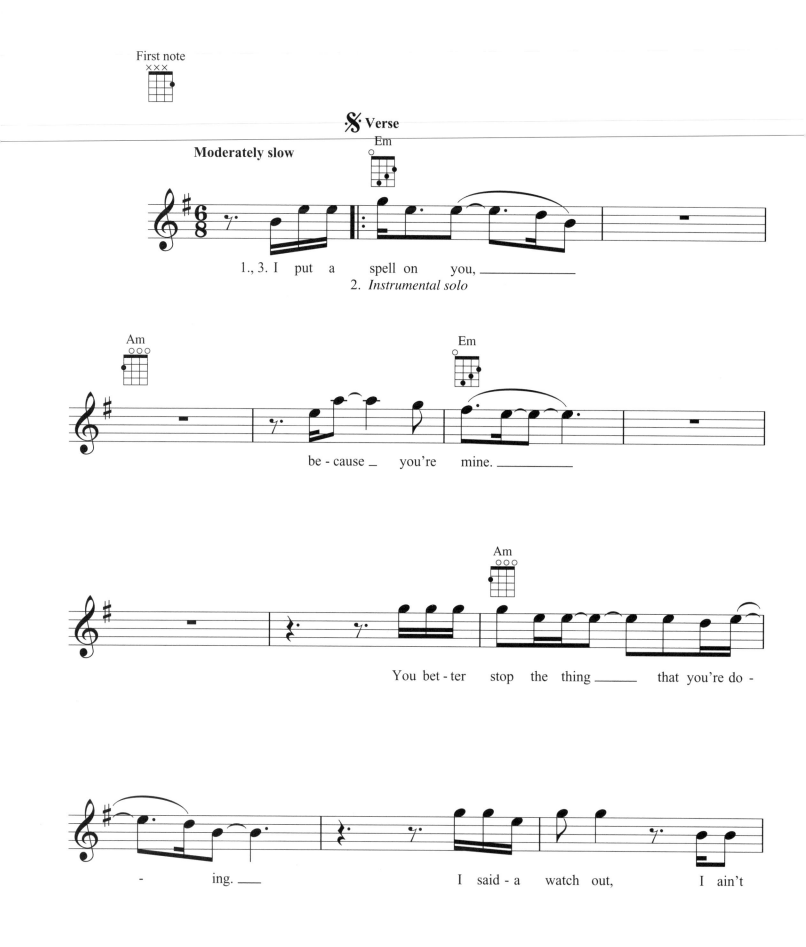

ly - in'. _____ Yeah! _____

I ain't gon - na take none of your _____

fool-ing a - round. _____ I ain't gon - na

take none of your _____ put-ting me down. _____ I put a

spell on you, _____

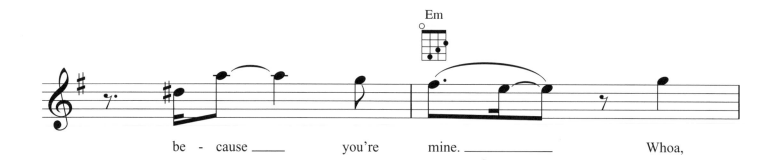

be - cause _____ you're mine. _____ Whoa,

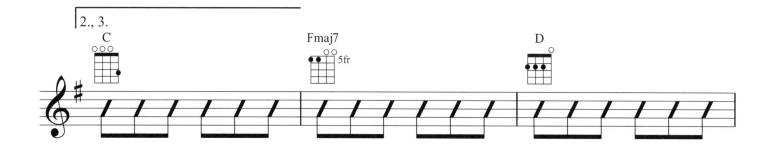

al - right!

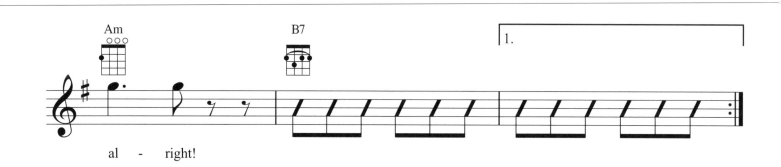

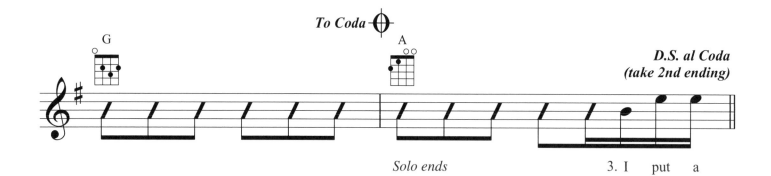

Solo ends                              3. I put a

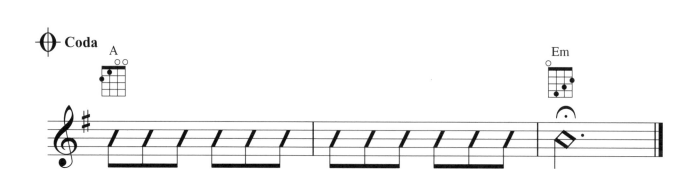

# I Heard It Through the Grapevine

Words and Music by Norman J. Whitfield and Barrett Strong

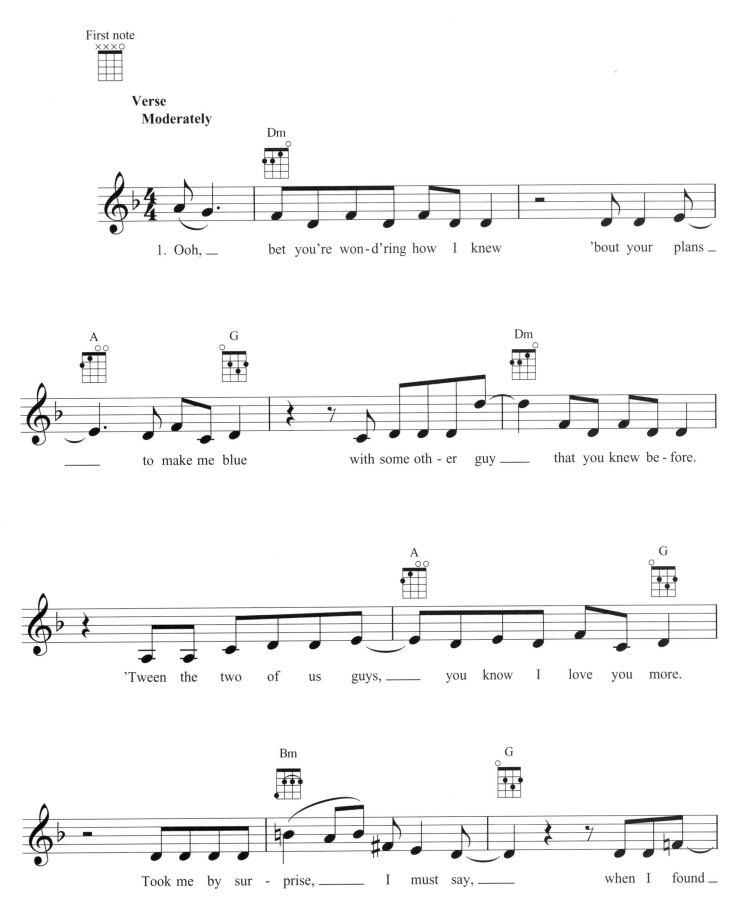

First note

Verse
Moderately

1. Ooh, __ bet you're won-d'ring how I knew 'bout your plans __ to make me blue with some oth-er guy __ that you knew be-fore. 'Tween the two of us guys, __ you know I love you more. Took me by sur-prise, __ I must say, __ when I found __

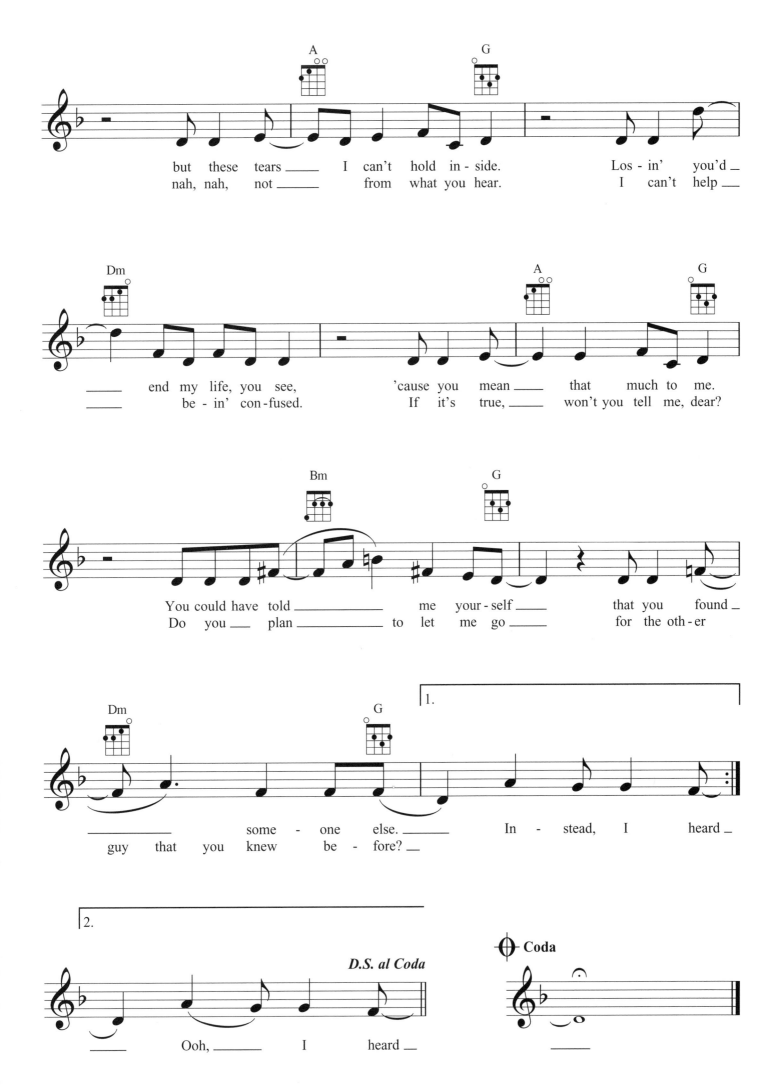

# Keep On Chooglin'

**Words and Music by John Fogerty**

got to ball ____ and have ____ a good time, ____ and

that's what I _____ call choo - gl - in'. ____

1., 2.

____ Keep on choo -

3.

**Outro-Chorus**

E7

Keep on choo - glin', keep on choo -

- glin', keep on choo - glin', choo -

- glin', choo - glin'.

*Additional Lyrics*

2. Here comes Mary, lookin' for Harry.
   She gonna choogle tonight.
   Here comes Louie, works in the sewer, Lord.
   He gonna choogle tonight.

3. If you can choose it, who can refuse it?
   You gotta choogle tonight.
   Go on, take your pick, right from the get-go.
   Y'all be chooglin' tonight.

# Long as I Can See the Light

**Words and Music by John Fogerty**

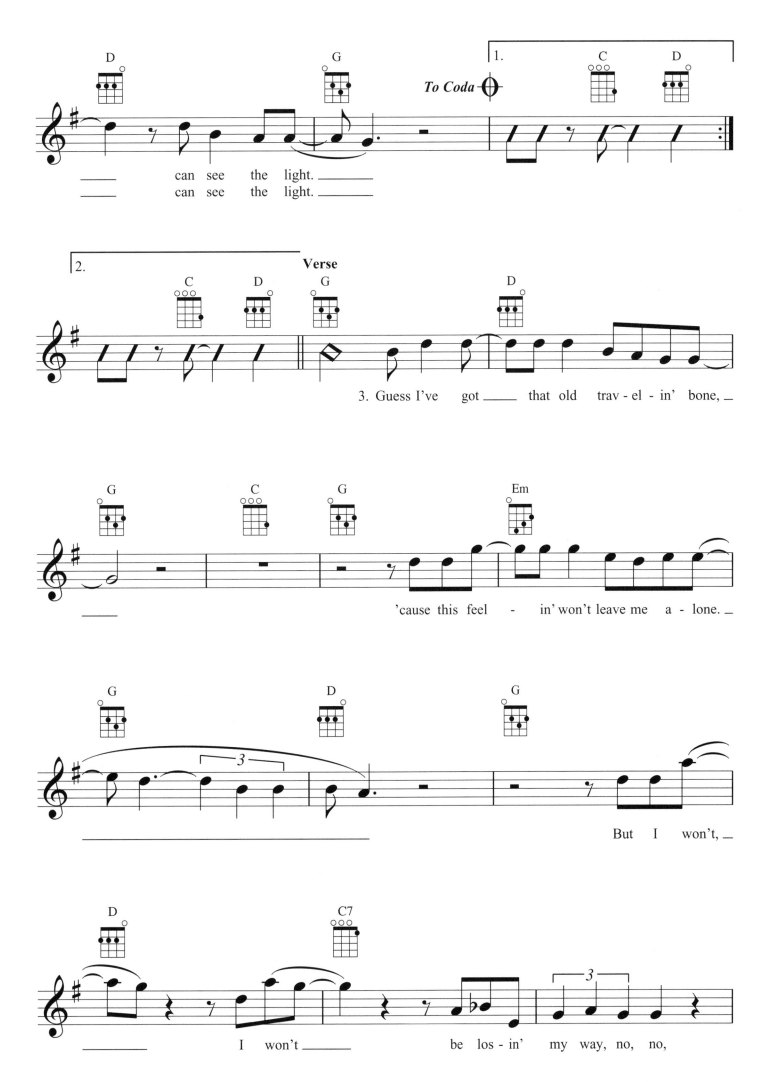

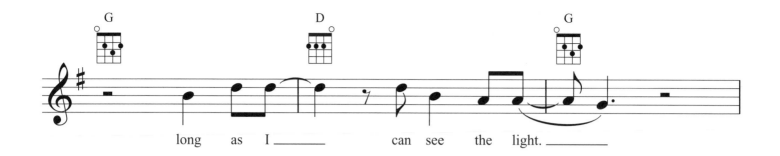

long    as    I _____    can    see    the    light. _____

**Interlude**

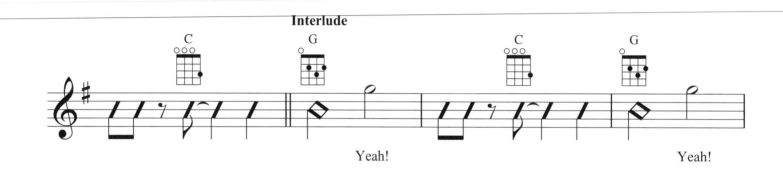

Yeah!                         Yeah!

Yeah!                         Oh,   yeah!

***D.C. al Coda***      Coda               **Outro**

Long    as    I \_\_

***Repeat and fade***

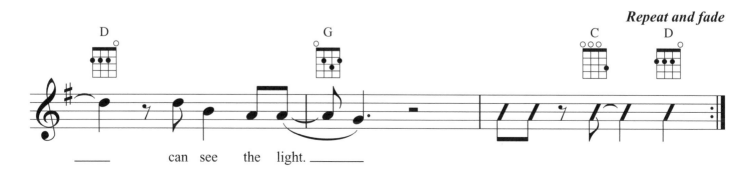

_____    can    see    the    light. _____

# Lodi

**Words and Music by John Fogerty**

First note

**Verse**
**Moderately**

1. Just a - bout a year a - go, _____ I

(2., 3.) *See additional lyrics*

set out on the road, _____ seek - ing my fame and for -

- tune and look - ing for a pot of gold. ___ Well,

things got bad, __ and things got worse; _ I guess you know the tune. _

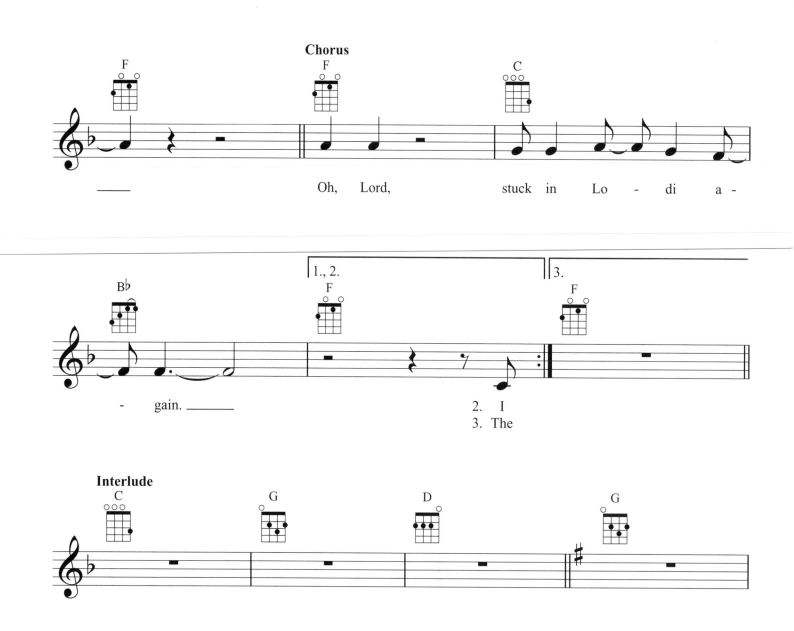

**Chorus**

Oh, Lord,     stuck in Lo - di a -

- gain. _____

2. I
3. The

**Interlude**

**Verse**

4. If I on - ly had a dol - lar     for

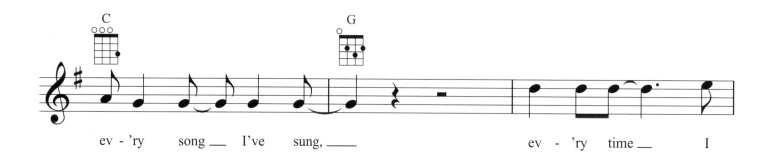

ev - 'ry song ___ I've sung, _____     ev - 'ry time ___ I

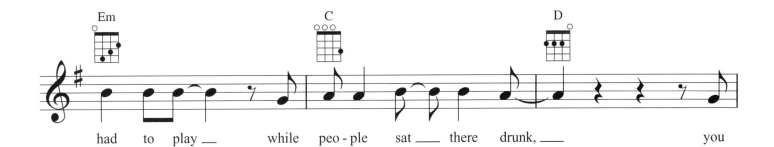

had to play ___ while peo - ple sat ___ there drunk, ___ you

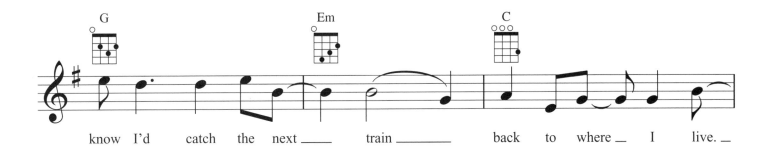

know I'd catch the next ___ train _____ back to where ___ I live. ___

**Outro-Chorus**

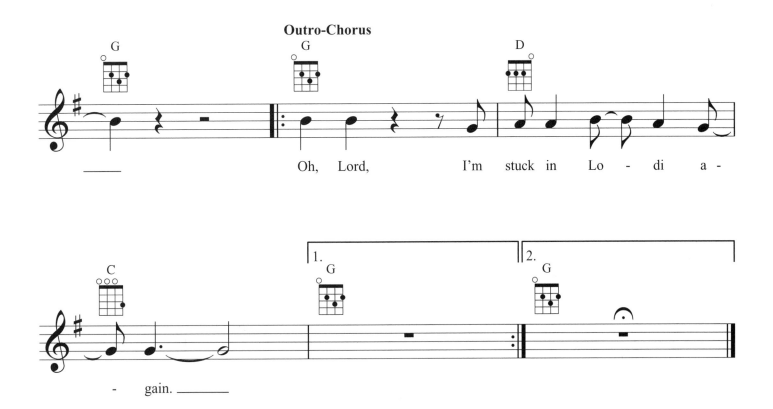

___ Oh, Lord, I'm stuck in Lo - di a-

- gain. _____

*Additional Lyrics*

2. I rode in on the Greyhound; well, I'll be walking out if I go.
   I was just passing through; must be seven months or more.
   I ran out of time and money; looks like they took my friends.

3. The man from the magazine said I was on my way.
   Somewhere, I lost connections; I ran out of songs to play.
   I came into town a one-night stand; looks like my plans fell through.

# Lookin' Out My Back Door

**Words and Music by John Fogerty**

# Proud Mary

**Words and Music by John Fogerty**

First note

**Verse**

**Moderate Rock**

1. Left a good job ___ in the cit - y,
2., 3. *See additional lyrics*

work - in' for the man ev - 'ry night and day, ___

and I nev - er lost one min - ute of sleep - in',

wor - ry - in' 'bout the way things might have been. ___

**Chorus**

Big wheel keep on turn - in', Proud ___

Mar - y keep on burn - in'. Roll -

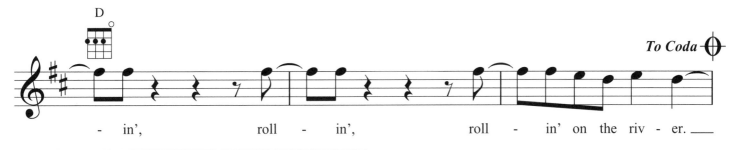

*To Coda*

- in', roll - in', roll - in' on the riv - er. ___

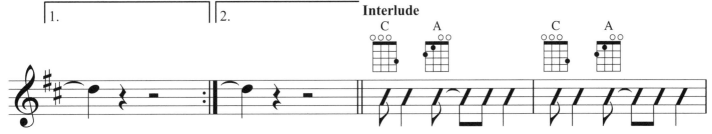

**Interlude**

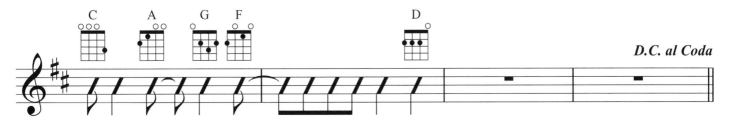

*D.C. al Coda*

**Outro**

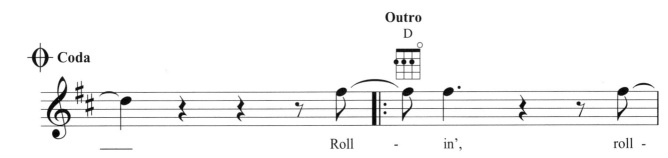

*Coda*

Roll - in', roll -

*Repeat and fade*

- in', roll - in' on the riv - er. ___ Roll -

*Additional Lyrics*

2. Cleaned a lot of plates in Memphis,
   Pumped a lot of 'pane down in New Orleans,
   But I never saw the good side of the city,
   Till I hitched a ride on a riverboat queen.

3. If you come down to the river,
   Bet you gonna find some people who live.
   You don't have to worry 'cause you have no money.
   People on the river are happy to give.

# Run Through the Jungle

**Words and Music by John Fogerty**

# Susie-Q

**Words and Music by Dale Hawkins, Stan Lewis and Eleanor Broadwater**

# Up Around the Bend

**Words and Music by John Fogerty**

1. There's a place up a-head and I'm go-in'
2.–4. *See additional lyrics*

just as fast as my feet can fly.

Come a-way, come a-way, if you're go-in',

leave the sink-in' ship be-hind.

**Chorus**

Come on the ris - in' wind. _____ We're

go - in' up _____ a - round the bend, _____ ooh. _____

1.–3.

4.

_____ yeah!

**Outro**

Doot, _

_____ doot, do, _ do.

*Repeat and fade*

Doot, _____ doot, do, _ do, do.

*Additional Lyrics*

2. Bring a song and a smile for the banjo.
   Better get while the gettin's good.
   Hitch a ride to end of the highway
   Where the neons turn to wood.

3. You can ponder perpetual motion,
   Fix your mind on a crystal day.
   Always time for a good conversation,
   There's an ear for what you say.

4. Catch a ride to the end of the highway
   And we'll meet by the big red tree.
   There's a place up ahead and I'm goin'.
   Come along, come along with me.

# Who'll Stop the Rain

**Words and Music by John Fogerty**

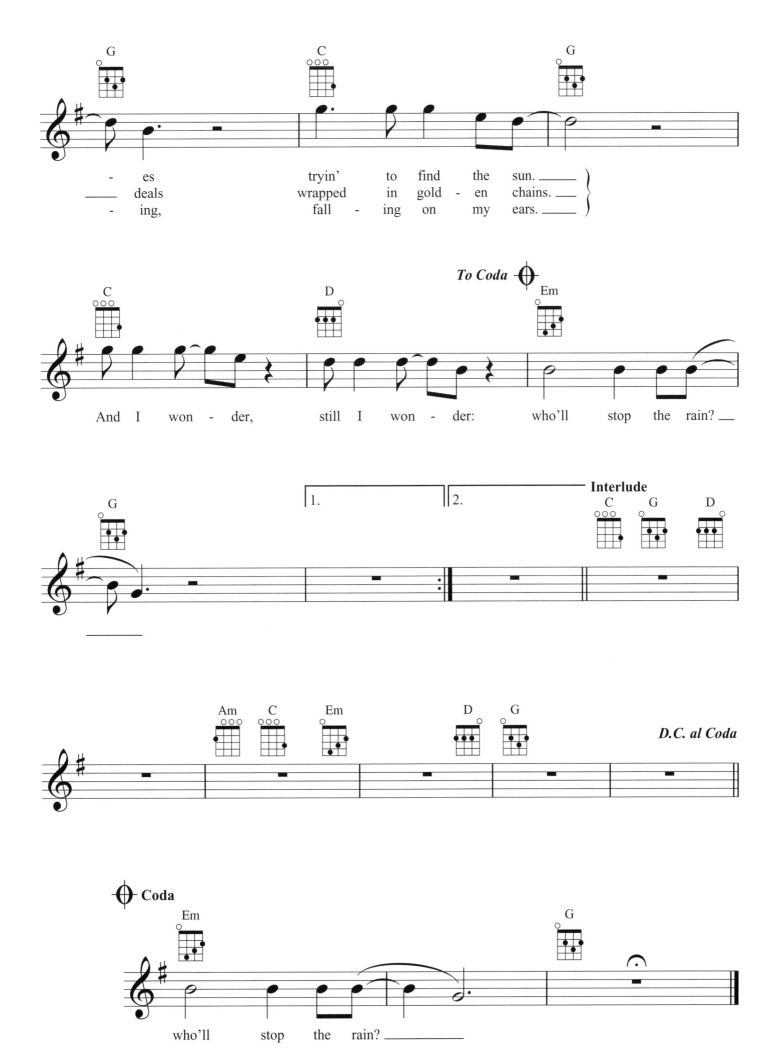

# Travelin' Band

**Words and Music by John Fogerty**

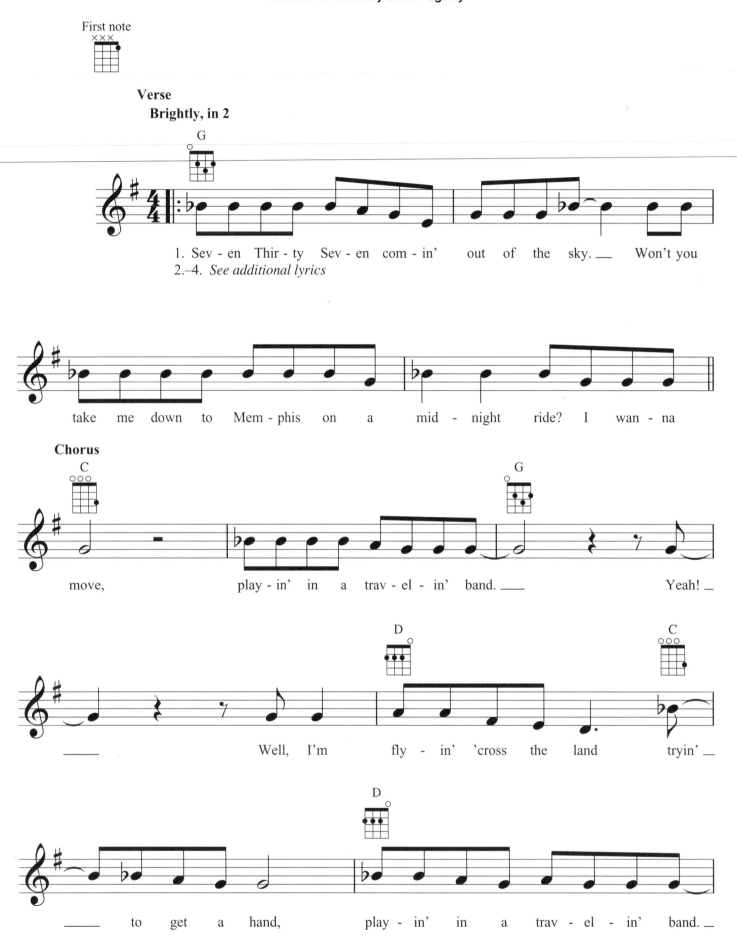

First note

Verse
**Brightly, in 2**

1. Sev - en Thir - ty Sev - en com - in' out of the sky.___ Won't you
2.–4. *See additional lyrics*

take me down to Mem - phis on a mid - night ride? I wan - na

**Chorus**

move, play - in' in a trav - el - in' band.___ Yeah!___

___ Well, I'm fly - in' 'cross the land tryin'___

___ to get a hand, play - in' in a trav - el - in' band.___

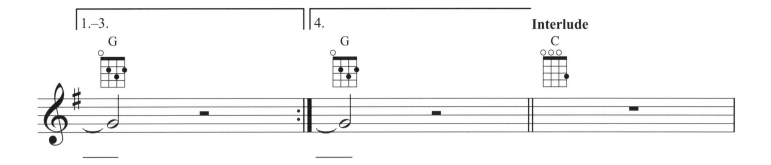

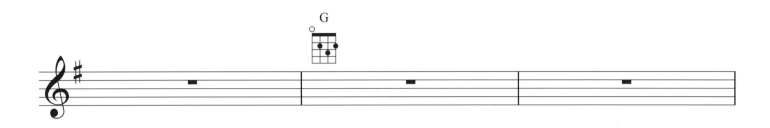

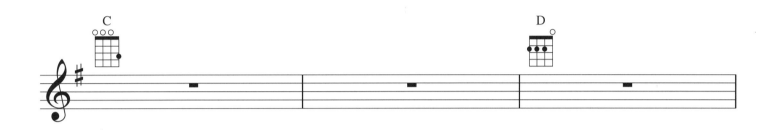

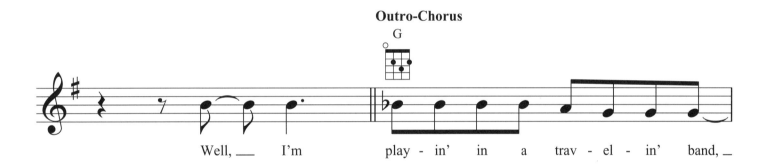

Well, ___ I'm     play - in' in a trav - el - in' band, ___

play - in' in a trav - el - in' band. ___

Want to give my - self a hand. _____     Well, I'm

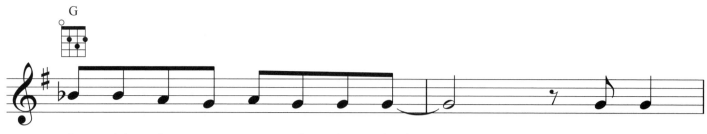

play - in' in a trav - el - in' band. _____ Well, I'm

fly - in' 'cross the land, tryin' _____ to get a hand,

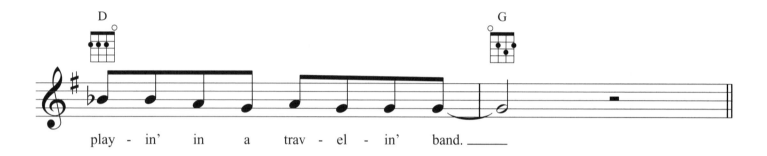

play - in' in a trav - el - in' band. _____

**Outro**

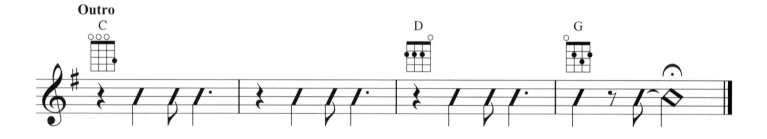

*Additional Lyrics*

2. Take me to the hotel, baggage gone, oh well.
   Come on, come on, won't you get me to my room?

3. Listen to the radio, talkin' 'bout the last show.
   Someone got excited, had to call the state militia.

4. Here we come again on a Saturday night
   With your fussin' and your fightin'. Won't you get me to the rhyme?